LION VS. KOMODO DRAGON

Gareth Stevens
PUBLISHING

By Janey Levy

Please visit our website, www.garethstevens.com. For a free color catalog of all our high-quality books, call toll free 1-800-542-2595 or fax 1-877-542-2596.

Cataloging-in-Publication Data

Names: Levy, Janey.
Title: Lion vs. komodo dragon / Janey Levy
Description: New York : Gareth Stevens Publishing, 2019. | Series: Bizarre beast battles | Includes glossary and index.
Identifiers: LCCN ISBN 9781538219331 (pbk.) | ISBN 9781538219317 (library bound) | ISBN 9781538219348 (6 pack)
Subjects: LCSH: Lion–Juvenile literature. | Komodo dragon–Juvenile literature.
Classification: LCC QL737.C23 L49 2019 | DDC 599.75'5–dc23

First Edition

Published in 2019 by
Gareth Stevens Publishing
111 East 14th Street, Suite 349
New York, NY 10003

Copyright © 2019 Gareth Stevens Publishing

Designer: Katelyn E. Reynolds
Editor: Monika Davies

Photo credits: Cover, p. 1 (lion) Pablo77/Shutterstock.com; cover, p. 1 (komodo dragon) Kit Korzun/Shutterstock.com; cover, pp. 1–24 (background texture) Apostrophe/Shutterstock.com; pp. 4–21 (lion icon) A_lion_A/Shutterstock.com; pp. 4–21 (komodo dragon icon) Miceking/Shutterstock.com; pp. 4, 6 (map on right) vectorEps/Shutterstock.com; p. 5 Dennis W Donohue/Shutterstock.com; p. 6 (map on left) NURWANNA WAEYUSOH/Shutterstock.com; p. 7 Richard Susanto/Shutterstock.com; p. 8 Andrew Paul Deer/Shutterstock.com; pp. 9, 13, 17, 21 (komodo dragon) Sergey Uryadnikov/Shutterstock.com; p. 10 adennis26win/Shutterstock.com; p. 11 Gerhard Zinn/EyeEm/Getty Images; p. 12 creativex/Shutterstock.com; p. 14 Mogens Trolle/Shutterstock.com; pp. 15, 19 GUDKOV ANDREY/Shutterstock.com; p. 16 Alta Oosthuizen/Shutterstock.com; p. 18 Eric Isselee/Shutterstock.com; p. 21 (lion) Volodymyr Burdiak/Shutterstock.com.

Printed in the United States of America

CPSIA compliance information: Batch #CS18GS: For further information contact Gareth Stevens, New York, New York at 1-800-542-2595.

CONTENTS

Words in the glossary appear in **bold** type the first time they are used in the text.

LETHAL LIONS

Lions are carnivorous, or meat-eating, big cats that mostly live in sub-Saharan Africa. A few live in northwest India. Male lions, with their beautiful manes, are known as the "king of beasts." Female lions are smaller, but they're also powerful predators.

Unlike other cats, lions live in groups, which are called prides. They hunt their **prey**, guard their territory, and raise their young with their pride. Lions also rest—a lot. These big cats spend up to 21 hours a day resting!

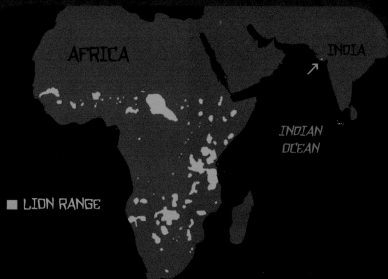

AFRICA

INDIA

INDIAN OCEAN

■ LION RANGE

MALE LIONS ARE SOMETIMES CALLED THE "KING OF THE JUNGLE." BUT THAT'S NOT WHERE LIONS LIVE. THEY PREFER TO LIVE IN THICK GRASSLANDS OR OPEN WOODLANDS.

5

KILLER KOMODO DRAGONS

Komodo dragons are carnivorous lizards that live on only a few islands in Indonesia, a country in Southeast Asia. These **reptiles** are the largest lizards in the world! They have a heavy body with short, stubby legs and a long, strong tail. Their flat head holds a snakelike, forked tongue.

Komodo dragons don't move very fast and spend their afternoons napping. But don't be fooled. These reptiles are scary predators that have even attacked people!

INDONESIA

■ KOMODO NATIONAL PARK

INDIAN OCEAN

AUSTRALIA

KOMODO DRAGONS ARE NAMED AFTER ONE OF THE ISLANDS WHERE THEY'RE FOUND. LOCALS CALL KOMODO DRAGONS "ORA," WHICH MEANS LAND CROCODILE.

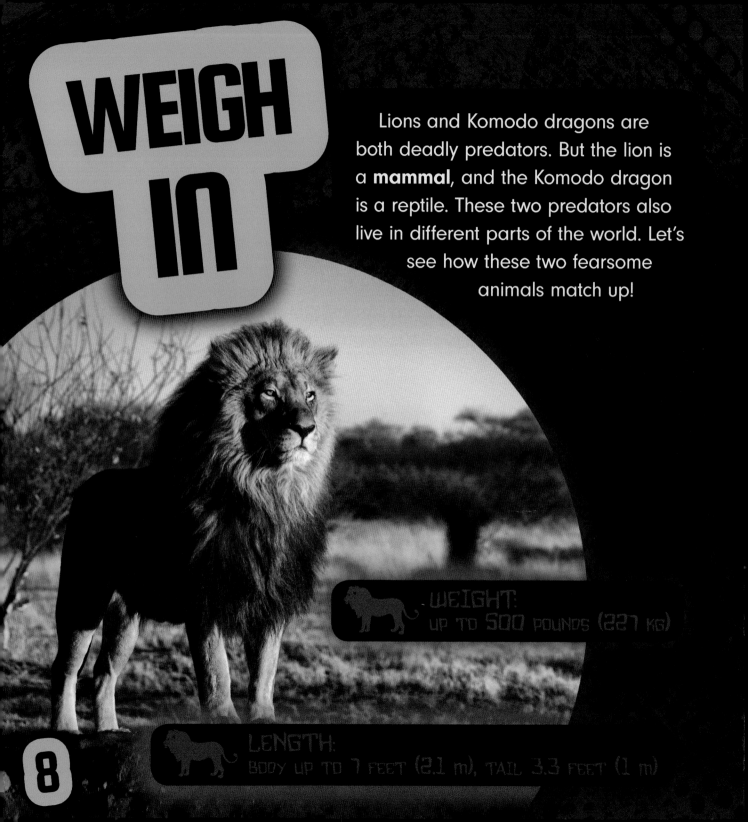

WEIGH IN

Lions and Komodo dragons are both deadly predators. But the lion is a **mammal**, and the Komodo dragon is a reptile. These two predators also live in different parts of the world. Let's see how these two fearsome animals match up!

WEIGHT:
UP TO 500 POUNDS (227 KG)

LENGTH:
BODY UP TO 7 FEET (2.1 m), TAIL 3.3 FEET (1 m)

LENGTH:
UP TO 10 FEET (3.1 m) FROM NOSE TO TAIL

WEIGHT:
UP TO 300 POUNDS (136 KG)

The Komodo
dragon has a
longer body than the
lion. But, the lion can weigh
more than one and a half times as much as
the Komodo dragon. Who wins this round?

TERRIBLE TEETH AND CLAWS

Lions have 30 sharp teeth for ripping and tearing their prey apart. The lion's strong claws hold down its prey as it eats.

LION'S CLAWS:
UP TO 3 INCHES (7.6 cm) LONG

LION'S TEETH:
CANINE TEETH AROUND 2.8 INCHES (7 cm) LONG

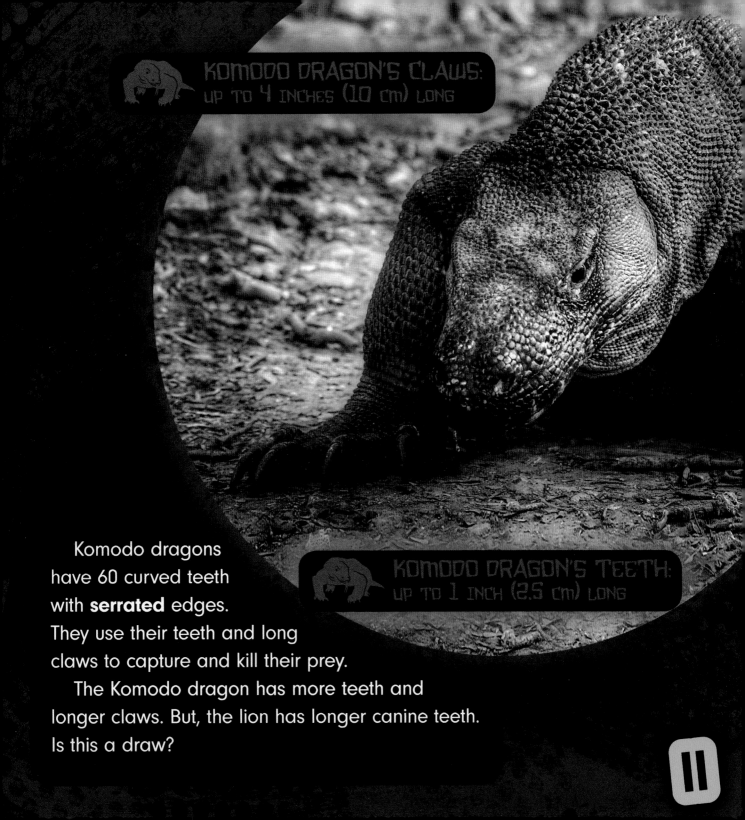

KOMODO DRAGON'S CLAWS:
up to 4 inches (10 cm) long

KOMODO DRAGON'S TEETH:
up to 1 inch (2.5 cm) long

Komodo dragons have 60 curved teeth with **serrated** edges. They use their teeth and long claws to capture and kill their prey.

The Komodo dragon has more teeth and longer claws. But, the lion has longer canine teeth. Is this a draw?

DEADLY BITE

Lions have a weaker bite than other big cats. But, their bite doesn't have to be extremely strong. Lions kill by squashing their prey's throat so it can't breathe.

LION'S BITE FORCE:
ABOUT 1,000 POUNDS PER SQUARE INCH

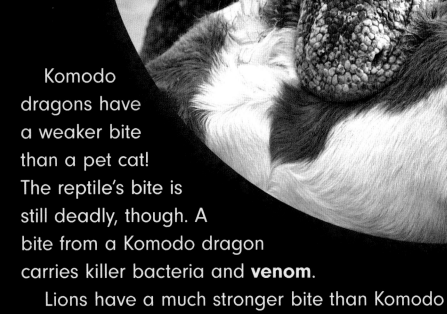

Komodo dragons have a weaker bite than a pet cat! The reptile's bite is still deadly, though. A bite from a Komodo dragon carries killer bacteria and **venom**.

Lions have a much stronger bite than Komodo dragons. But both bites are equally deadly!

13

FULL SPEED AHEAD

Usain Bolt, the world's fastest human, hit a top speed of 27.8 miles (43 km) per hour in a short race. Lions can run even faster, but they don't have much **stamina**. They can only run at top speed for about 157 feet (48 m).

LION'S TOP SPEED:
up to 35 miles (56 km) per hour

14

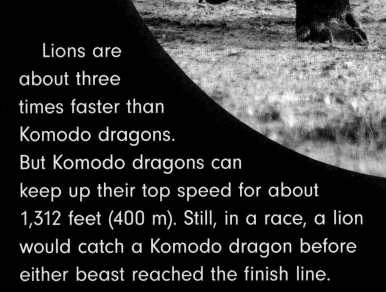

Lions are about three times faster than Komodo dragons. But Komodo dragons can keep up their top speed for about 1,312 feet (400 m). Still, in a race, a lion would catch a Komodo dragon before either beast reached the finish line.

ON THE HUNT

Female lions do most of the hunting for prides. Working in groups, they can catch prey as large as elephants! Male lions hunt alone. Lions also steal prey from other predators.

LION'S HUNTING METHODS:
* STALK THEIR PREY, OFTEN AT NIGHT
* MALE LIONS AMBUSH THEIR PREY, USING THEIR STRENGTH TO CATCH THE ANIMAL

Komodo dragons tend to live and hunt alone. They can kill large animals such as water buffalo. They're also scavengers, which means they eat the remains of dead animals. Sometimes, a Komodo dragon will even eat another Komodo dragon!

17

WASTE NOT, WANT NOT

After lions kill their prey, they settle down to eat. Lions don't eat all parts of their prey. They don't eat the skeleton or other parts that are hard for them to **digest**.

LIONS EAT UP TO 75 PERCENT OF THEIR PREY

An animal
may escape a
Komodo dragon
attack only to die
days later from the
venom and bacteria in the
Komodo's bite. The Komodo
dragon will eat almost all of its prey,
including the bones, hide, guts, and hoofs!

The Komodo dragon wins this battle,
as they make better use of their prey.

19

AND THE WINNER?

Now that you've learned more about these two deadly predators, who do you think would win if they battled to the death? The lion has a longer body and is a faster runner. This mammal also has long canine teeth and a strong bite. But, the Komodo dragon weighs more and has a greater number of teeth. And, this reptile's bite carries deadly bacteria and venom.

It looks as if these two scary carnivores are evenly matched. You decide who would win if this mammal and reptile were to meet in battle!

 THIS BIZARRE BEAST BATTLE WOULD NEVER ACTUALLY HAPPEN. THE LION AND KOMODO DRAGON LIVE IN COMPLETELY DIFFERENT PARTS OF THE WORLD. BUT WE CAN STILL IMAGINE!

GLOSSARY

ambush: to attack from a hiding place

camouflage: colors or shapes in animals that allow them to blend with their surroundings

canine: a long, pointed tooth near the front of the mouth

digest: to break down food inside the body so that the body can use it

mammal: a warm-blooded animal that has a backbone and hair, breathes air, and feeds milk to its young

prey: an animal that is hunted by other animals for food

reptile: an animal covered with scales or plates that breathes air, has a backbone, and lays eggs, such as a turtle, snake, lizard, or crocodile

serrated: having sawlike points along an edge

stalk: to hunt an animal by following it quietly and carefully

stamina: the strength needed to do something for a long time

venom: something an animal makes in its body that can harm other animals

FOR MORE INFORMATION

BOOKS

Hirsch, Rebecca E. *Komodo Dragons: Deadly Hunting Reptiles*. Minneapolis, MN: Lerner Publishing Group, 2016.

Joubert, Dereck and Beverly Joubert. *Face to Face with Lions*. Washington, DC: National Geographic, 2010.

Sherman, Jill. *Komodo Dragons*. North Mankato, MN: Capstone Press, 2017.

WEBSITES

Komodo Dragon
kids.nationalgeographic.com/animals/komodo-dragon/
Get to know the Komodo dragon better with this overview of the world's largest lizard!

African Lion: King of Cats
kids.sandiegozoo.org/animals/african-lion
Discover more about the "king of cats" with these fun lion facts.

INDEX